D0801680

Happy

60th

Birthday

Happy 60th Birthday

A Book of Wit and Wisdom

Edited by Susan Feuer

Illustrated by Haing Soon Lee

Ariel Books

Andrews McMeel Publishing

Kansas City

 For information write Andrews McMeel Publishing, an Andrews McMeel Universal company, 4520 Main Street, Kansas City, Missouri 64111.

www.andrewsmcmeel.com

ISBN: 0-8362-6791-5

Library of Congress Catalog Card Number: 98-84240

Happy

60th

Birthday

So, here it is—your sixtieth birthday. Somehow it seems that people celebrating their sixtieth birthdays get a bit cheated. A big fuss is made over fortieth birthdays, and then an even bigger fuss is made a decade later with the coming of the fiftieth. Despite being as important a landmark as other birthdays, the sixtieth is often overlooked. Well, it's time that the big six-oh got its due.

What does turning sixty mean? Different things to different people, of course. But hopefully, at age sixty, you will have more time to yourself than you've had for decades. Your sixties should be an era in which you take care

of yourself and do the things *you* want to do—whether that means retirement, a second job, new hobbies, traveling, or pressuring your kids to have children.

So enjoy this special birthday and celebrate yourself for making it to sixty.

The age of a woman doesn't
mean a thing. The best
tunes are played on the
oldest fiddles.

Sigmund Engel

Your outlook, your frame of
mind, as you advance in years
is what matters most.

Garson Kanin

To me, old age is always fif-
teen years older than I am.

Bernard Baruch

I grow more intense as I age.

Florida Scott-Maxwell

When men reach their sixties and retire, they go to pieces. Women just go right on cooking.

Gail Sheehy

Autumn is mellower, and what we lose in flowers, we more than gain in fruits.

Samuel Butler

It takes a long time to become a person.

Candice Bergen

My yesterdays walk with me. They keep step; they are faces that peer over my shoulder.

William Golding

If you don't want to get old,
don't mellow.

Linda Ellerbee

We grow neither better nor
worse as we get old, but more
like ourselves.

May Lamberton Becker

The years between fifty and seventy are the hardest. You are always being asked to do things, and you are not yet decrepit enough to turn them down.

T. S. Eliot

I grow old ever learning
many things.
Solon

We don't grow older; we
grow riper.
Pablo Picasso

You can take no credit for
beauty at sixteen. But if you
are beautiful at sixty, it will be
your soul's own doing.

Marie Stopes

From the ages of thirteen
to fifty, society places
women in a defined role.
At fifty, we leave it, and at
sixty, we've completed the
transition. Assuming that
we have a little security,
we are now totally free to
be ourselves. We're back

to that stage of being a
little girl of nine or ten,
who can climb trees and
be autonomous. . . . But
we have our own
apartments.

Gloria Steinem

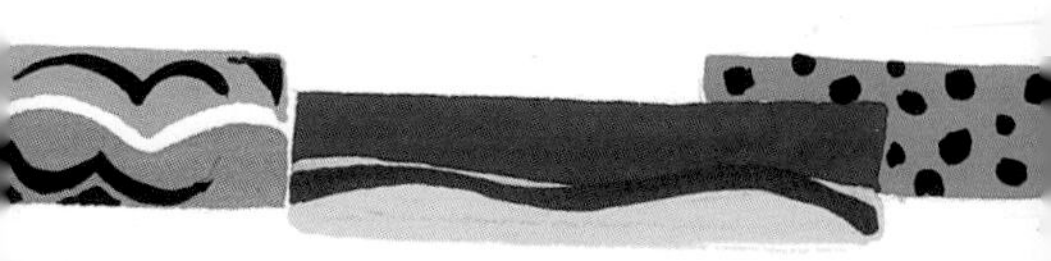

The lines, the wrinkles . . . let them get deeper, particularly the laugh lines. That's not only what gives life its savor, it's the thing that charges our batteries.

Hume Cronyn

I must confess, with sixty only around the corner, that I have found existence on this planet extremely amusing, and, taking one day with another, perfectly satisfactory. If I had my life to live over again, I don't think I'd change it in any particular of the slightest consequence.

H. L. Mencken

How unnatural the imposed view . . . that passionate love belongs only to the young.

May Sarton

The spiritual eyesight
improves as the physical
eyesight declines.

Plato

An energetic middle life is, I think, the only safe precursor of a vitally happy old age.

Vida D. Schudder

The belief that youth is the happiest time of life is founded upon a fallacy. The happiest person is the person who thinks the most interesting thoughts, and we grow happier as we grow older.

William Lyon Phelps

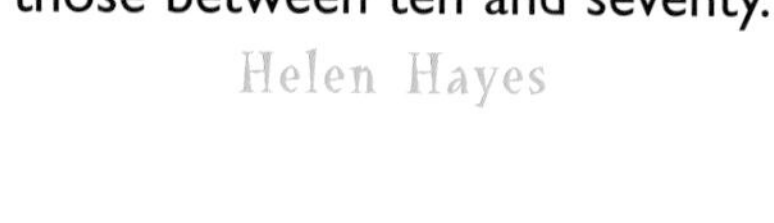

The hardest years in life are
those between ten and seventy.

Helen Hayes

Retirement must be wonderful.
I mean, you can suck in your
stomach for only so long.

Burt Reynolds

Youth is happy because it has
the ability to see beauty.
Anyone who keeps the
ability to see beauty never
grows old.

Franz Kafka

At sixty, you might come
back; at seventy, they think
you are gaga.

Sir Harold Wilson

At ten, a child; at twenty, wild;
At thirty, tame, if ever;
At forty, wise; at fifty, rich;
At sixty, good, or never.

Anonymous

1. Never lose interest in life and the world.
2. Eat sparingly and at regular hours.
3. Take plenty of exercise but not too much.
4. Get plenty of sleep.
5. Never allow yourself to become annoyed.

6. Set a daily schedule of life and keep it.
7. Get a lot of sunlight.
8. Drink as much milk as will agree with you.
9. Obey your doctor and consult him often.
10. Don't overdo things.

John D. Rockefeller's rules for life, which he wrote at age sixty

Middle age is when, whenever you go on holiday, you pack a sweater.

Denis Norden

In youth, we learn; in age,
we understand.

Marie von Ebner-Eschenbach

At middle age, the soul
should be opening up like
a rose, not closing up like
a cabbage.

John Andrew Holmes

I like that word [sexagenarian]. It has a ring to it. A ring of excitement and élan. And, alas, of promise.

Goodman Ace

In mirrors and especially in photographs, I notice that I have grown old. But it is what is young in me that notices it. It is a young man who sees an old one. He is amazed—without bitterness and with respect, the way youth

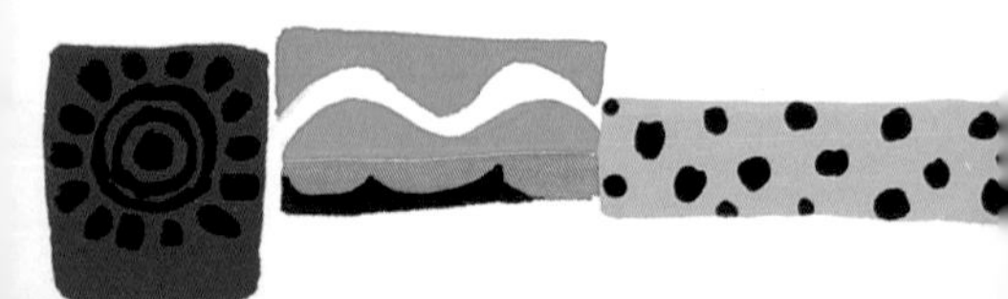

regards old age among noble peoples. . . . My youth respects my old age. My old age protects my youth. That is why I am at peace.

Jean Cocteau

Now that I am sixty, I see why
the idea of elder wisdom has
passed from currency.

John Updike

Keep working as long as you can. Remember, you can't help getting older, but you don't have to get old. . . . There's an old saying, "Life begins at forty." That's silly—life begins every morning when you wake up. Open your mind to it; don't just sit there—do things.

George Burns

Just remember, once you're over the hill, you begin to pick up speed.

Charles M. Schulz

A new year is a clean slate, a chance to suck in your breath, decide all is not lost, and give yourself another chance.

Sarah Overstreet

Now I'm over sixty, I'm veering toward respectability.

Shelley Winters

Maturing men and women must avoid ruts, fixed habits, old ways. The antidote to aging is action, both physical and mental, and learning.

Garson Kanin

With sixty staring me in the face,
I have developed inflammation of
the sentence structure and a defi-
nite hardening of the paragraphs.

James Thurber

It began in mystery, and it will end in mystery, but what a savage and beautiful country lies in between.

Diane Ackerman

Age is strictly a case of mind over matter. If you don't mind, it doesn't matter.

Jack Benny

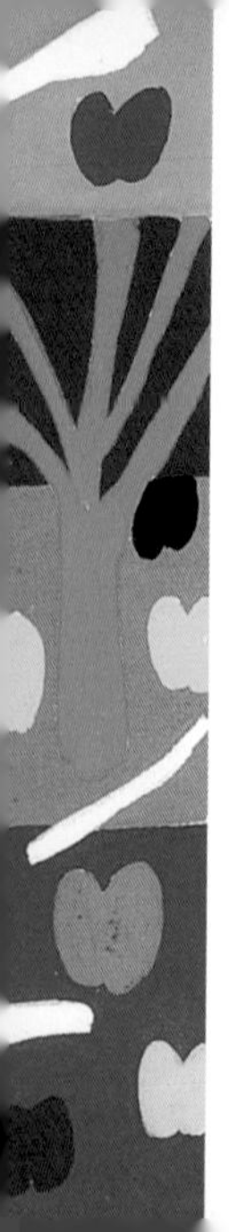

In the last few years,
everything I'd done up to
sixty or so has seemed
very childish.

T. S. Eliot

There is more felicity on
the far side of baldness
than young men can
possibly imagine.

Logan Pearsall Smith

Do not deprive me of my age. I have earned it.

May Sarton

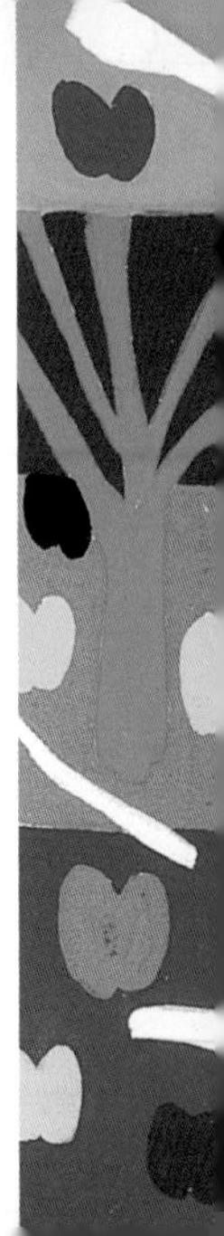

I'm sixty-five. I'll be sixty-six in January. What should I do? Shoot myself? I've never worried about age. If you're extremely, painfully frightened of age, it shows. Life doesn't end at thirty. To me age is a number, just a number. Who cares?

Jeanne Moreau

As I get older, my interests multiply rather than lessen in number.

John Cage

It is a mistake to regard age as a downhill grade toward dissolution. The reverse is true. As one grows older, one climbs with surprising strides.

George Sand

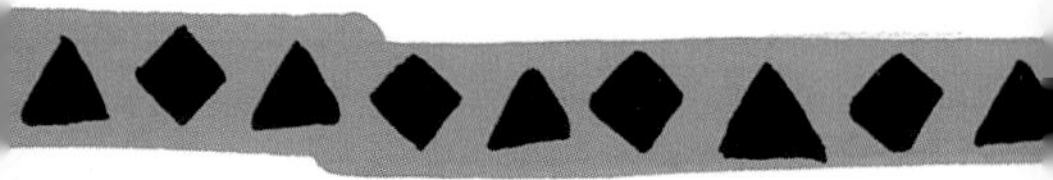

From thirty-five to forty-five women are old, and at forty-five, the devil takes over, and they're beautiful, splendid, maternal, proud. The acidities are gone, and in their place reigns calm. They are worth going out to find, and because of them some men never grow old. When I see them, my mouth waters.

Jean-Baptiste Troigros

It's not how old you are
but how you are old.

Marie Dressler

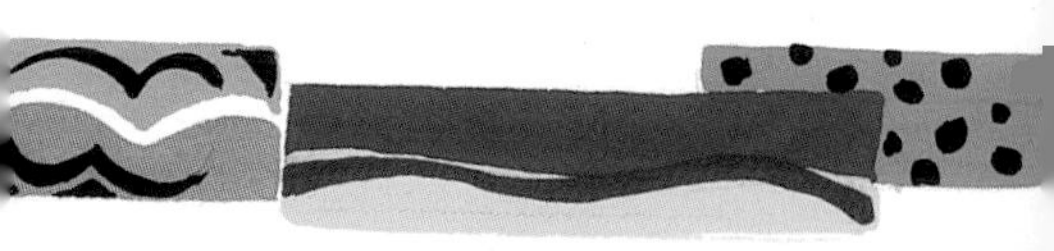

You're never too old to
become younger.

Mae West

Middle age is when you're
faced with two temptations
and you choose the one that
will get you home by nine
o'clock.

Ronald Reagan

Let us respect gray hairs,
especially our own.

J. P. Senn

Do you count your birthdays
thankfully?

Horace

We "become" twenty-one, "turn" thirty, "push" forty, "reach" fifty, "make it" to sixty, and "hit" seventy. If we reach one hundred, we're likely to revert to childhood, proudly adding fractions to the numbers.

Larry Miller

The young are slaves to dreams; the old, servants of regrets. Only the middle-aged have all their five senses.

Hervey Allen

One of the signs of passing youth is the birth of a sense of fellowship with other human beings as we take our place among them.

Virginia Woolf

I am luminous with age.

Meridal Le Sueur

In this country, some people start being miserable about growing old while they are still young.

Margaret Mead

I have always felt that a woman has the right to treat the subject of her age with ambiguity until, perhaps, she passes into the realm of over ninety. Then it is better she be candid with herself and with the world.

Helena Rubinstein

Middle age is when anything new in the way you feel is most likely a symptom.

Laurence J. Peter

Youth is not a question of years;
one is young or old from birth.

Natalie Clifford Barney

Setting a good example for your children takes all the fun out of middle age.

William Feather

Youth supplies us with colors,
age with canvas.

Henry David Thoreau

Nobody grows old by merely living a number of years. People grow old only by deserting their ideals.

Douglas MacArthur

Perhaps one can at last in
middle age, if not earlier, be
completely oneself. And what
a liberation that would be!

Anne Morrow Lindbergh

I never expected to have, in
my sixties, the happiness that
passed me by in my twenties.

C. S. Lewis

My eyes have seen much, but they are not weary. My ears have heard much, but they thirst for more.

Rabindranath Tagore

Anyone who stops learning is old,
whether at twenty or eighty.
Anyone who keeps learning stays
young. The greatest thing in life is
to keep your mind young.

Henry Ford

To know how to grow old is the
masterwork of wisdom, and one
of the most difficult chapters in
the great art of living.

Henri-Frédéric Amiel

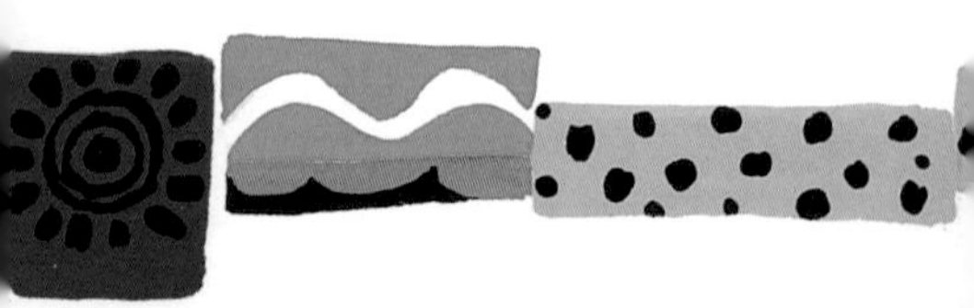

One of the many things nobody ever tells you about middle age is that it's such a nice change from being young.

Dorothy Canfield Fisher

One starts to get young at the age of sixty.

Pablo Picasso

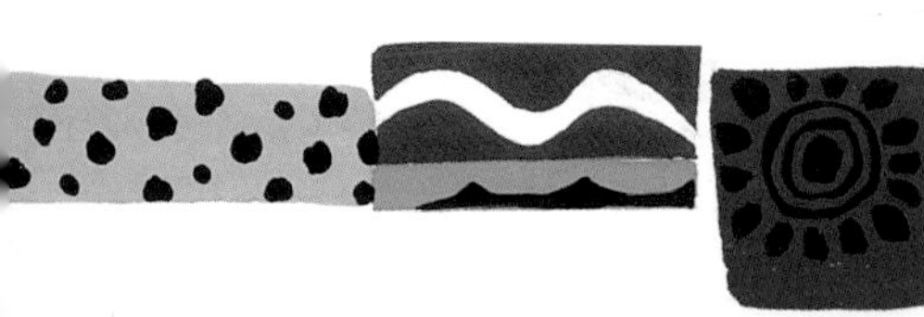

Middle age—by which I mean anything over twenty and under ninety.

A. A. Milne

It is not the years in your life
but the life in your years that
counts.

Adlai Stevenson

We are happier in many ways when we are old than when we were young. The young sow wild oats. The old grow sage.

Winston Churchill

Within I do not find wrinkles and
used heart, but unspent youth.

Ralph Waldo Emerson,
at age sixty-one

To the Chinese, the sixtieth birthday is quite a big deal—the most revered of all birthdays. This has to do with the Chinese astrological system of twelve animals (Rat, Ox, Tiger, Rabbit, Dragon, Snake, Horse, Ram, Monkey, Rooster, Dog, and Pig) and five elements (wood, fire, earth, metal, and water). Every year is assigned an element and an animal; for

example, you could have been born under the sign of the Dragon in a fire year or under the sign of the Monkey in a wood year. The exact combination of animal and element repeats itself only once every sixty years, which is why the Chinese consider sixty to be such a special year (assuming that practically no one lives to age 120).

Gifts for the Sixtieth Birthday

- A gorgeous, expensive watch (sixty seconds in a minute; sixty minutes in an hour)
- Five dozen roses
- A trip to China (since the Chinese celebrate and honor the sixtieth over all other birth-days)

- A sixty-day supply of something decadent: champagne, caviar, lobster, Belgian chocolate
- A copy of the Beatles' *Sgt. Pepper's Lonely Hearts Club Band* album (it contains the song "When I'm 64")
- An hour-long massage or facial

What Being Sixty Means

- It's been an entire decade since you got that invitation to join the AARP.
- Reduced ticket prices for muse-ums, the movies, airfare, plays, etc.
- Bifocals are so passé; now it's on to *tri*focals!
- Melatonin is your friend.

- Unlike the Baby Boomers, the Me Generation, or Generation X, you belong to a generation with no nickname.
- You buy sweaters for your dachshund.
- Your idea of a wild night is doing two shots of antacid before bed instead of your usual one.

designed and typeset by
Junie Lee in NYC